The Conflict Resolution Library™

Dealing with Bullying
Qué hacer con los bravucones

Marianne Johnston

Traducción al español:
Mauricio Velázquez de León

PowerKiDS press. & **Editorial Buenas Letras**™
New York

Published in 2008 by The Rosen Publishing Group, Inc.
29 East 21st Street, New York, NY 10010

First Bilingual Edition

Book Design: Lissette González

Photo credits: Cover by Seth Dinnerman; p. 4 Shutterstock.com; p. 19 © istockphoto.com/Jelani Memory; all other photos by Seth Dinnerman.

Cataloging Data

Johnston, Marianne.
   Marianne Johnston / Dealing with bullying; traducción al español: Mauricio Velázquez de León.
   p. cm. – (Conflict Resolution Library/Biblioteca solución de conflictos)
Includes index.
   ISBN-13: 978-1-4042-7658-1 (library binding)
   ISBN-10: 1-4042-7658-0 (library binding)
1. Bullying–Juvenile literature. [1. Bullying. 2. Spanish language materials.] I. Title. II. Series.

Manufactured in the United States of America

Contents

Contenido

Do you know someone who seems to enjoy hurting others? Maybe there is someone like that at your school. Someone who **intimidates** and hurts others is a bully.

¿Conoces a alguien que parezca disfrutar asustando o haciendo daño a los demás? Tal vez haya alguien así en tu escuela. Un bravucón es alguien que **intimida** y lastima a los otros.

5

Some bullies scare people with their fists. Others scare people with their words. Many bullies use **threats** or insults to scare people or to make them feel bad. A bully who uses words can be just as mean and scary as one who uses fists.

Algunos bravucones asustan a las personas con sus puños. Otros lo hacen con sus palabras. Muchos bravucones usan **amenazas** o insultos para asustar a los demás. Un bravucón que usa palabras puede ser tan malvado como uno que usa sus puños.

Bullies act the way they do for different reasons. Sometimes someone is being mean to them. So they treat others the same way. Other bullies think that if they show everyone how tough they are, no one will know how scared or lonely they are.

Los bravucones actúan de esta manera por muchas razones. A veces alguien ha sido malvado con ellos. Entonces ellos tratan de la misma manera a los demás. Otros piensan que, al demostrar lo fuertes que son, nadie sabrá que tienen miedo o que se sienten muy solos.

Most bullies have low **self-esteem**. They hurt and insult other people to make themselves feel better. Sometimes bullies are jealous of other people's **accomplishments**. They don't feel that they are good at anything.

La mayoría de los bravucones tienen muy baja **autoestima**. Como no se gustan mucho a sí mismos, entonces lastiman e insultan a otras personas. Algunas veces, los bravucones están celosos de los **logros** de las otras personas. Creen que no son buenos para nada.

A bully wants you to get angry or to fight with him. Walk away from the bully. If he still bothers you, tell him firmly to leave you alone. If this doesn't work, tell a grown-up.

Lo que un bravucón quiere es que te enojes, o pelear contigo. Cuando esto suceda, trata de alejarte de él. Si sigue molestándote, dile con firmeza que te deje en paz. Si esto no funciona, habla con un adulto.

Do you bully other people? Think about why you do it. Maybe someone is bullying you. Maybe you're not happy with yourself. Maybe you're scared that other people won't like you. Try talking to a adult. That grown-up may be able to help you.

¿Eres de los que intimidan a los demás? Si es así, piensa por qué lo haces. Tal vez alguien te esté intimidando a ti. Tal vez tengas miedo de no gustarle a los demás. Trata de hablar con un adulto. Un adulto puede ayudarte.

If you see a bully giving someone a hard time, try to help. Don't try to fight the bully. Stand up for the person being bullied. There is strength in numbers. When there is more than one person, the bully will most likely back off.

Si ves a un bravucón haciéndole pasar un mal rato a alguien, trata de ayudar. No intentes pelear con él. Trata de apoyar a la persona a la que está molestando. Tu ventaja está en los números. Cuando hay más de una persona, lo más probable es que el bravucón se retire.

If a person has been a bully, she probably doesn't have many friends. Being kind to a bully will help her feel better about herself. Bullies are just like everyone else. They want to be liked and accepted too.

Si una persona ha sido bravucona por mucho tiempo probablemente no tenga muchos amigos. Ser amable con un bravucón lo hará sentirse mejor consigo mismo. Los bravucones son como cualquier otra persona. Ellos también quieren ser aceptados y gustarle a los demás.

Marco was the school bully. Carlos saw him bullying a kid. Carlos decided to help. He calmly told Marco to leave the kid alone. When Marco threatened him, Carlos did not fight back. Marco saw that he was outnumbered and left.

Marco era el bravucón de la escuela. Un día, Carlos lo vio molestando a un chico. Carlos decidió ir a ayudar. Con calma le dijo a Marco que dejara en paz al chico. Cuando Marco lo amenazó, Carlos no respondió. Marco se vio superado y decidió alejarse.

The next day, Carlos talked to Marco at school. The boys learned that they lived near each other. They started walking to school together and soon became friends. Marco felt a lot better now that he had a friend to talk to.

Al día siguiente, Carlos vio a Marco en la escuela. Al platicar, se enteraron de que vivían muy cerca. Empezaron a caminar juntos a la escuela y, muy pronto, se hicieron amigos. Marco se siente mucho mejor ahora que tiene un amigo con quien platicar.

Glossary

accomplishments (uh-KOM-plish-mint) Things that have been done with skill, knowledge, or ability.

intimidates (in-TIM-ih-dayt) Makes someone afraid.

self-esteem (SELF-es-TEEM) Feeling good about yourself.

threats (THRET) Statements of what will be done to hurt someone.

Glosario

amenaza (la) Dar a entender a alguien que lo vas a lastimar.

autoestima (la) Sentirte bien contigo mismo.

intimidar Causar miedo a las personas.

logro (el) Algo que ha sido hecho con habilidad, conocimiento o destreza.

Index

Índice